Copyright 2013

Designed by
Cynthia Albright-Parrish

Illustrated by
Jaime Andrews

Dedicated to my children and grandchildren who
inspire me daily! Thank you with all my heart -
Greg, Heather, Georgia, Will, Jay, Claire, Alex,
Fritz, Katie, Ryan, Sayre, and Hollen
And
In memory of my wonderful father
William Hollen Keeling M.D.
December 24, 1918-May 8, 1963

You have wonderful dreams for this precious child!
Hold this baby close to comfort and nurture. May this book
be helpful to teach, bond, entertain and show your love and
affection. Be certain your little one hears sweet and encouraging
words daily. Make books and reading to one another a special
part of every day!

This child will amaze you with an eagerness to learn.
Encourage this from the beginning. Your reassuring voice and
gentle touch will create a world of trust, love and
understanding, and a happy, loving relationship
to treasure forever.

Wishing you the best,

-Cindy-

This Book Belongs to _____

_____ is adventurous, adorable, affectionate, amazing, artistic, beautiful, cherished, considerate, creative, cuddly, curious, cute, delightful, dependable, determined, enchanting, enthusiastic, exceptional, fabulous, fantastic, funny, gentle, giggly, handsome, happy, helpful, imaginative, important, incredible, joyous, kind, lively, lovable, magical, marvelous, magnificent, mischievous, musical, neat, nifty, nice, original, outstanding, patient, peppy, polite, precious, pretty, quick, quiet, refreshing, sensational, sensitive, silly, smart, smiling, special, splendid, spirited, sweet, talkative, terrific, unique, vivacious, wiggly, witty, wonderful, young, zany and zippy!

Playful Ideas

Use the Rhythm of Language in many different ways -
Try a variety of playful fun voices - spirited, quiet, squeaky!
Make up Stories - Name the Characters!
Point out Page Numbers and Colors
Teach Beginning Sounds of words!
Help Little Ones Choose their Favorite Pages!
Encourage the child to read and embellish the story -
sing the words!
GIGGLE, LAUGH, CUDDLE and HAVE FUN!!

Aa

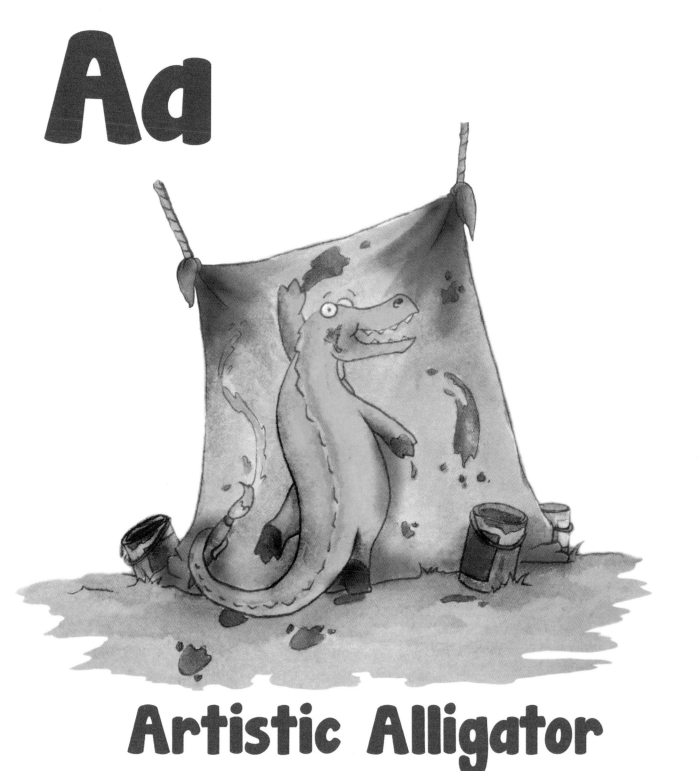

Artistic Alligator

Bb

Beautiful Busy Babies

Cc

Curious Cat

Celebrating Centipedes

Dd

Dependable Dump Truck

Ee

Enchanting Elephant

Ff

Fabulous Funny Fish

Gg

Giggling Goose

Gentle Giraffe

Hh

Happy Helpful Horse

Ii

Imaginative Igloo

13

Jj

Joyous Juggling Jester

Kk

Kind Koala

Lively Lovable Lion

Magical Mermaid

Nn

Neat Night Owl with Nuts

Oo

Outstanding Octopus

Pp

Patient Penguin, Pig, and Panda

Qq

Quiet Queen

Rr

Refreshing Raindrops

Ss

Silly Snowman

Tt

Talkative Turtle

Uu

Unique Unicorn

Vv

Vivacious Violin

Ww

Witty Wiggly Worm

Xx

eXciting Xylophone

Yy

Young Yaks

Zz

Zany Zippy Zebra

My Mommy, Daddy, _____ is

Affectionate, Blessed, Calm, Considerate, Dependable, Empathetic, Expressive, Fun, Gentle, Generous, Genuine, Honest, Honorable, Imaginative, Important, Intelligent, Joyful, Kind, Loving, Loyal, Listening, Musical, Neat, Optimistic, Patient, Polite, Quick, Responsible, Relaxed, Reassuring, Skillful, Sensitive, Smart, Talkative, Terrific, Thoughtful, Trustworthy, Understanding, Versatile, Wise, XXXXX (kisses), Youthful,
Zany and Zippy!

Made in the USA
Lexington, KY
21 August 2014